A Father's
Responsibility

A Father's *Responsibility*

DR. SHARON FORDE-ATIKOSSIE

CITIOFBOOKS, INC.
3736 Eubank NE Suite A1
Albuquerque, NM 87111-3579
www.citiofbooks.com
Hotline: 1 (877) 389-2759
Fax: 1 (505) 930-7244

Ordering Information:
Quantity sales. Special discounts are available on quantity purchases by corporations, associations, and others. For details, contact the publisher at the address above.

Printed in the United States of America.

ISBN-13:   Paperback   979-8-90124-162-2
              eBook   979-8-90124-163-9

Library of Congress Control Number: 2026908208

DEAR READERS,

As I looked at the picture with my son and his child, I saw the love and compassion and immediately asked myself what type of gift can I give both of my sons for Father's Day, and to let both sons know that "I see them".

I did not want to constantly tell them" let us go to church or let us go to lunch or dinner" but to give them something to remind them of who they are, and their responsibility as fathers.

I wanted them and any other father to have something special.

Hope they will be curious to know what is written in this book, and with God's grace every word that is written absorbs in them and any other father who reads it, as they continue to be not only responsible fathers, but true men of God

Dr. Sharon Forde Atikossie.

No child wants to
hear their father say no……
except when …..

And

All children want to hear

their father say yes….

Except…… when…..

"Mom I cannot wait to go home to my kids"

"Mom I am going to protect my child with my life"

"Mom, the baby thinks she is a queen, but have me up all night and now is fast asleep during the day"

"Mom these children keep me busy, and I love them so much"

"Mom the baby is rolling"

"Mom the baby got their first teeth"

"Mom the baby took the first step"

"Mom the baby is saying Dada – tears came to my eyes"

"Mom the baby is trying to climb the stairs!"

"Mom the baby is walking"

"Mom the baby is talking"

"Mom the baby would not stop talking"

O God mom this child is not listening to anything I say, only if dad was here"

A mother cannot help smiling when her sons make these comments especially the last comment which brings the statement to <u>mind!</u> "pay back!

Our family lived in a one-way street where the neighbors are of old, and retired people, five young boys to include my sons and three young lads lives in this street.

This was a place where the young men lived sheltered life, and the outside world seems to have more influenced over them than the homes we live in.

I learned that their behavior at home was the behavior of angels. They cannot seem to do no wrong, but when they are out of the house there was a vast difference in their behavior (We learn about this through the people who knew us, and to be honest it was hard to believe, until we witness their behavior ourselves, and I am aware that many parents experience this

For this is one reason, my husband and I learn not to say "we would place our head on the chopping block for our children"

With this in mind all of these young men became single fathers bringing each parent to wander where we went wrong with them especially when each household had prayers and praises every day.

Most of us were pastors, deacons, or elders in our churches, aiming to set a godly example for our children. This is not to imply that those who do not serve God lack such intent.

All these young men became proud fathers, always talking about "I am a father" of course with having the broad smile on their faces with their chest stretch up very high, however none of them realized at that moment as Myles Monroe put it bluntly "having a child is no guarantee that you are a father. Simply means that you are a male creature. A father is somebody that's hard to find", he also notes that " it doesn't take a man to have a child. It only takes a male"

None of these young men realized that while they are rejoicing we the parents was wandering where we went wrong, asking ourselves the question "does these kids know what they are getting themselves into? and to be frank they were not listening to the advised given to them.

We the parents had to figure out a way to talk to our sons as grown men, and not children because now that they have responsibilities, still living at home, not paying any rent, still want to act like little children, and grown up at the same time, and goes to the point that they do not want to hear the advises given because they suddenly knows better than we the parents.

When it was time to have a sit-down conversation, for us my husband chose a time to have a one and one conversation without myself and later included me.

QUESTIONS TO THE SON

Many questions were asked and of course all the boy can say is that they are having a child.

Question: Who is the girl

Answer: Her name is…..

Question: How old is she

Answer: I don't know

Question: Where she comes from

Answer: I don't know

Question: Did you meet her parents

Answer: No (this is when all smiles went from their faces)

Question: Now that you are having a child when are you getting married?

Answer: Married! I did not say I am getting married, all I am saying I am getting a child

Question: Well, where are you going to live

Answer: Live? I have a home here (this is where there seems to be confusion on their faces)

Statement —Since you are an adult now, you will have to find your own home

Reply: Just because I told you I am having a child, you are now throwing me out.

Father's final statement: "I am not the one who allow weakness to defeat discipline!"

Of course, mom is saying nothing while the head of the household speaks but thinking "what others would say" since we are supposed to be the leaders in the churches where we are trying to lead by example, and is teaching the importance of marriage, and responsibilities about sex before marriage!

WHAT OR WHO IS A FATHER

The Merriam-Webster dictionary describes a father as male parent; a man who has begotten a child or a male animal who has sired an offspring" (one who shows up and clap the loudest and longest)

And!

He is that man, not boy who has to stand form

He is that man who have responsibilities

He is that man who must make sure that his household is in good condition.

He is that man who has to provide

He is that man who has to make decision

He is that man who the children look up to

He is that man who is being relied on

He is that man who need to be respected!

What is the importance of a father

A father gives their children a sense of identity

A father gives their children a sense of legitimacy

A father gives their children a sense of family

A father gives their children a sense of purpose

A father gives their children a sense of destiny

A father gives their children a sense of heritage

A father gives their children a sense of ethics

A father gives their children "Not just father love, but shows them a sense of responsibility"

A father's responsibility extends far beyond provision, encompassing emotional presence, mentorship, and unconditional love that shapes a child's character. Key themes include being a role model, sacrificing for the family's well-being, and active involvement in the child's daily life.

When it comes to a father who has given their life to Jesus Christ there is the understanding that they have already learn and understand their responsibilities because they already learn and understand the responsibility of their heavenly father.

This is not to say that those fathers who are not saved does not understand their responsibilities.

A father who is saved and all other fathers need to know the Heavenly Father and understand that unique love that they learn.

This is when they need to share and show their child how they should live.

It is said that it takes a village to train a child, and since this is so in order for the father to function in a Godly manner for nothing is wrong for fathers to seek advice from their mentors and advisors.

Every father needs a spiritual father, and spiritual mentor.

As stated in 1 Corinthians 4:15, "Though you may have ten thousand instructors in Christ, yet you do not have many fathers."

Every father first needs to be a good man as stated in 1 Kings 2:2 and 1 Corinthians 13:11 that there is a need to be mature.

While the fathers continue to focus on their responsibility of their child, they must remember that:

the boy child are passive, while they are responsible the boy child's lives for the moment, while the father plans for the future the boy speaks while the father acts,the boy child demands while the father serves.

In Malachi 4:6 says that this something God will do, "He will turn the hearts of the fathers to the children" for God wants fathers to turn their hearts toward their children.

The father who is godly will love and respect the mother of their child.

While the father loves and cares for his children, he must remember to also provide, show love and care; discipline, and not forgetting to pray for their child.

A father's love is not enough for a child. His love must be added with responsibility in order for a child to have a normal life

This does not mean that the child may turn out to be successful, however the father still has the responsibly to do the best he can with his child.

FATHER CONFRONTING ONESELF

Fathers who are proud to have their children confront challenges and barriers.

When they examine themselves, they would want to make changes to themselves so that they can be the best parents because that is what is expected of them.

They would then want to fix these barriers regardless of their situations regardless of their economic, psychological, or social status,

When this is done, after finishing fixing themselves, fathers as one would say "would greatly affect their children's development through various path, either direct or indirect.

DIFFERENT CULTURE

Culture plays a great part in a man's life, and every father grows up differently even though they may be living in the same home.

Each one of them has their own way of doing things when it comes to surviving, and because of this the way of taking care of their child would be different.

In most cultures the man is the head of the household, and because of this there is that common denominator of the way they treat their kids.

Relationship between father and child

In most cases you will see the difference in treatment of how the father relates to their boy child and their girl child.

The girl child is pampered as if they are queens, and the boy is treated in a manly manner so that they can become the protector as they should be.

In the case of the girl child, A father would treat his baby girl with protective, attentive love, acting as her first model for any relationships; he would also provide emotional security and affection and (abondance of kisses, and hugs, while the boy mostly get hugs and handshakes).

Again, in the case of the girl, he would often express this through consistent, hands-on care, such as bathing, feeding, and singing to her, while fostering her self-worth, confidence, and emotional development.

He would engage himself in daily care routines, playing, cuddling, spending one-on-one time together show how active and involve he is to include showing his affection.

He would establish a sense of physical and emotional safety, which builds trust, thereby providing security and protection.

He would be very emotionally expressive, attentive, and responsive to a daughter's cries or needs, when it comes to emotional responsiveness.

He would be developing a behavior of respect, thereby respecting the child's mother, as he sets the standard for how his daughter is expecting to be treated by him.

He would build his girl child self-esteem by telling her she is beautiful, capable, and loved, which would help her develop confidence.

There is that bond that they both share which would often shape the daughter's future relationships, self-worth, and emotional intelligence.

Normally for the father, the girlchild from baby to adult would cling to their father for security and emotional support, and the actions of the father will be to show his child what a good relationship with a man should be like.

If a father is loving and gentle, his daughter will look for those qualities in men when she's old enough to begin dating. If a father is strong and valiant, she will relate closely to men of the same character.

They model their relationships with others based on their father's character; boys behave the same way that their father's behave.

The boy child will seek approval from their fathers from a very young age, and this is due to the constant communication they have between them.

They will grow up imitating the behavior, and when the father is absent, the young boy will look to other male figures to imitate

In the case of the boy child, the father would treat his baby boy by fostering independence through rough and tumble plays, thereby building resilience, and providing a secure, protective presence.

He would encourage confidence; acts as a male role model, and bonds through hands-on care like bathing, feeding, and physical affection.

I learn that the key aspects of a father's approach are physical engagement and play, this is where the fathers often engage in more physical, high-energy, or "rough-and-tumble" play.

This is something which is believe to help boys learn to manage various situations.

The father should take the initiative to reach out to the child, despite the pain in their heart, and the father having that feeling of being a failure.

The father will have that doubtful feeling that the child would not want to visit because they feel that the child may be disappointed or ashamed of him.

The father must try to be long distant fans by continuously cheering the child on in everything that they are doing

They must reach out, by showing them love while assuring them that they are not responsible for them being in prison.

The father should take the initiative to reach out to the child, despite the pain in their heart, and also having that feelings of being a failure.

They will have that doubtful feeling that the child would not want to visit because they feel that the child is disappointed or ashamed of him.

They must try to be long distant fans by continuously reaching out, by showing them love by telling them all the time while assuring them that they are not responsible for them being in prison.

Be honest with the child and have honest conversation, especially encouraging them that they should not be ashamed of their father.

He, the father must be honest with the child and have honest conversation, especially encouraging them that they should not be ashamed of themselves, or where they come from.

The father should encourage the boy child to take risks; explore their surroundings, and solve problems.

The father should also foster independence, hands-on care bonding with their child.

Also, when modern fathers are active in daily care such as changing diapers, bathing, and feeding, this is crucial for building a strong, secure, and affectionate bond.

In the case of role modeling and character, this is where fathers teach by example, demonstrating how to handle frustration, showing empathy, and acting with integrity.

Discipline and Structure is another of father's responsibility. They provide firm, consistent, and constant discipline combined with love, which helps sons understand boundaries and consequences, also there is the emotional Support, and this is where fathers provide a sense of security, and safety through their presence.

There are fathers who are just plain bread winners for the family only and their responsibility is just to go to work and take the money home, and ignore the family.

Sometimes life is beyond their control, and there is that feeling that if they work and support the family that is enough.

DIFFERENT TYPES OF FATHERS

I learned that there are many types of fathers, all of them have different styles and their parenting styles are also different, and these actions may form an impact on a child's self-esteem; their academic success, and their well-being, thereby bringing a balance between rules and nurturing.

This allows the father to make informed choices that would benefit their child's development, and it would also affect everything from your child's self-esteem to their academic success.

This authoritative style father comes with a combination of warmth and structure, thereby promoting "independence while maintaining clear expectations"

This style also comes with the way of the father's treatment towards the boy child, and how he treat the girl child, and all of this comes with love which is considered to be the most effective style for fostering happiness when raising a child.

This type of parenting affects children in many positive outcomes to include academic achievement, heightened self-esteem, and resiliency.

The children with authoritative parents seem to achieve positive outcomes that includes close relationships; nurturing relationships with parents; having the tendency to be responsible and respectful; having the ability to manage their aggression; getting a high degree of self-esteem, self-confidence and self-regulation.

It includes having children to be more likely to be happy and successful, and having the ability to clearly express their emotions.

The children who experience this is said to be trusted and is able to make the right decision on their own; to include having to be able to set high expectations for themselves; willing to perform well academically and socially, also include having a sense of balance in their lives.

Authoritarian father enforces strict rules, and expectations, valuing obedience over emotional support, and in this case the children may become obedient, but they lack self-esteem and social skills.

The parents focus on strict rules, obedience, and discipline. They have high expectations of the children with the notion of "do as I say and do not do as I do syndrome," and in this case they use punishment when their children do not follow their guidelines.

They go to the extent of making decision for their child while rarely giving the child any input in the matter, and thereby making the rules while enforcing the consequences with little or no regard of their child's opinion.

This can affect the child in many ways, such as their social skills; indecisiveness and trouble thinking on their own; poor judge of character; anger management and resentfulness; hostility and aggression and all of this can lead to rebelling on the children's part especially when there is outside influence which would seem better.

When it comes to permissive fathers, most children love them, because they are very lenient, and indulgent.

They give too much freedom to the child there by providing very little or no guidance and discipline allowing the child to have little or no self-control.

The Father would rule, and knowingly know that they would rarely enforce them; do nothing when the child needs discipline; has the feeling that their child will learn best with little interference from anyone, while allowing them to do what they want.

According to Dr. Warren who is a counselor he expressed that this kind of father "caters to their children's needs without giving much discipline"

"When they do use consequences, they may not stick to it, for the father will give privileges back if a child begs, or they may allow a child to leave time-out early if they promises to be good, and these permissive parents are the total opposite of strict parents.

In the case of neglectful fathers, or the non-involved father, their parenting would either be a father who is unable to take care of his child.

The father may have made the decision that he did not care, or deliberately did not want to take care of the child, and decided that he did not want to get involve.

He may be a father who do not want the responsibility for various reasons such as not prepared to be a father or he may be having the behavior which comes from is own father, and this induce influence can become more difficult as one would think.

Also, it can be either, taking on the responsibility of the child can be beyond their control, such as living far away from the child; being in prison where there is restrictions being placed on the father, or they may just plainly do not care.

This does not include a father who is jobless, for this type of father can still have influence over their child's life.

This behavior leads to negative outcomes, which can lead to lingering effects on the child's emotional and social development.

Looking at this situation, it is evident that there is a need for both parents to be in the child's life, for the instinct of a mother is different from the instinct of a father, however when both instincts come together, there will be the end result of an average behaved child.

This type of father does not or is unable to ask about the child's welfare, such as about their school, or their homework; or in most cases does not know where the child is.

In the case of a single father, they may not get the permission to see the child on a regular basis, causing them not to have full control of the child's behavior.

They are being able to spend little or no time with the child, and this father may have little or no rules or expectations for the child.

In the case of the father ignoring the child for various reasons while receiving little or no guidance, nurturing, or parental attention, or simply put they do not have set rules or "expectations, and they tend to have minimal knowledge about what their children are doing."

The uninvolved father expects the child to raise themselves, and they do not devote much time or energy to meeting the child's basic needs.

In some cases, the uninvolved father may lack knowledge about child development, or they may believe that their child will do better without their oversight.

These fathers may be neglectful but it's not always intentional. They may have mental health issues or substance abuse problems.

Other fathers may not be able to care for a child's physical or emotional needs consistently the way they want.

All of these things can affect the child, and without any guidance, structure, or parental involvement, children of neglectful parents often act out.

I learn that the child with uninvolved father have the worst outcomes, and they're more likely to experience things such as substance use; rebelliousness; delinquency (vandalism, assault, rape, petty theft); lower cognitive and emotional empathy, and diminished self-esteem.

As in the case of a father who is incarcerated, it also causes pain for both father and child. The father should take the initiative to reach out to the child, despite the pain in their heart, and also having that feeling of being a failure.

They will have that doubtful feeling that the child would not want to visit because they feel that the child is disappointed or ashamed of them.

They must try to be long distant fans by continuously reaching out, by showing them love, and by telling them all the time while assuring them that they are not responsible for them being in prison.

Be honest with the child and have honest conversations, especially encouraging them that they should not be ashamed of their father.

For the father who travels and is unable to stay at home regularly as in the case of Military personnel.

Fathers who communicate consistently have far better relationships than those who do not.

The children look forward to seeing their father, with the hope that he stays home a little longer.

Father's responsibility for children with physical challenges

When it comes to a father's responsibility for children with physical challenges, or with special needs, including a premature child as one would say "there is no shame in their game."

Patience! Patience! Patience!

is the key

They cannot do it alone. First of all, it is not what they were expecting while they were looking forward to seeing their child for the first time.

Their expectation was to get a healthy baby either boy or girl, and they are also looking forward for a football player for a boy, and a queen for a girl.

This would be the time the father would have to look to God for everything and seek his guidance. They would need to be humble, if not they would not only hurt themself, they will be hurting the child also.

Seek a lot of advice from the right people.

Find training on how to take care of and deal with the child

Find various support so that the father can get a breathing space.

This is the time the father will cry

This is the time the father will say "Why me",

This is the time when the father will have no choice but to watch your anger

And this is the time the father becomes very protective and shows a lot of love.

The father will mature a lot in many ways, and you would surprise yourself of your own strength, and this is the time you are to look to God.

As the musician Jelly Roy, sang the below song:

"When the weight of the world
Is heavy on me
When the night feels cold
And I can't find peace
I lift my eyes To the heavens above
You hold me close In Unfailing love.

Lord you are my strength
My song in the night
You carry my soul is
You fight All my fights
In you I will trust
Forever I'll stand
My refuge my Saviour
Holding my hand

When my spirit is weak
And I cannot go on

Your mercy reminds me
that I still belong

Your word is my life
My hope and my shiel
In your hold presence
My soul is heal

The father would make sure that their child gets the best treatment.

They would learn the child's behavior and try to anticipate their every move.

The protection of the child would be increased drastically

Their care for the child will be immeasurable.

The father would develop more patients

The child's needs will be met in every aspect

They would make sure that the child's needs are met in every aspect.

This is the time when the father engages in both spiritual and physical counseling and goes to the point of seeking various help from family and friends and join groups that facilitate parents with the same situation for these fathers often face high-stress, and emotional challenges, including financial pressures and potential relationship strain.

They are responsible for prioritizing self-care, building support networks, and maintaining open communication with partners is crucial for endurance, becoming a fierce advocate, finding joy in small moments, and redefining strength to embrace vulnerability.

In order to make life easy the father should seek advice for both themselves the child's mother on how to deal with their child; have a support system; find strength in their spouse.

The father will always be an advocate; have many quality time with the child; find many correct information on how to take care of the child; have many teachable moments; and make future plans.

PARENTS WITH A TROUBLED CHILD

The parents with a troubled child responsibility must still show love, they would experience fear, anger, and stress, but must continue to support that child despite their disappointment.

They will do their best to help that child, even if it is only through prayer.

Responsibility of the father for the child who seems not to care or do not want to listen.

In this case the father must have patience and try to eliminate anger when dealing with situations. Sometimes the father would make demands of the child instead of reasoning with them.

The father still must show love and kindness even though they may want to use the belt on the child.

They must focus on building a strong, loving, and consistent connection to foster positive change which includes using nonviolent, firm discipline, engaging in one-on-one time, acting as a positive role model, and, if necessary, seeking professional guidance for both the child and themselves.

The father must focus on building a secure relationship to help regulate behavior, rather than just using authority, which can often backfire when it comes to challenging children.

Remember that discipline should be fair and nonviolent, focusing on teaching rather than punishing.

Regularly participate in their child's life, including eating together, listening to them, and engaging in activities that they enjoy.

Demonstrate honesty, respect, and responsibility because these are the thing they want their child to foster.

Recognize that the father's own mental distress can impact a child; seeking help for personal issues can improve the child's environment.

Understand that if their child's behaviors are extreme or dangerous, look for professional help, such as therapy, counseling or coaching, in order to learn better management techniques.

Remember to avoid conflict and understand that failing to set boundaries can worsen behavioral issues, because the child would want to take the father for granted or not being very serious.

Try not to blame the child for all issues. This is the point where the father must pay attention to the child's feeling for they may be reacting to something other than the subject at hand.

The father should not dismiss the child's behavior as if nothing is wrong.

Being physically present but emotionally absent can leave a child feeling undervalued, and not forgetting to regain the child's trust, especially after conflict, which often requires rebuilding trust with the child's mother as well.

THE FATHER RESPONSIBILITY FOR THE CHILD GROWTH

When it comes to the child's growth the father must be active, in not only the child's growth but influencing; emotionally; cognitive; social; and physical development.

This can be done in various ways, such as taking the child to various places so that they can have hands on experience because the father's involvement will improve the child's academic success; self-esteem; and emotional stability.

All of these things bring a style that fosters security, self-confidence, and better self-regulation.

Being a single father

When it comes to a single father, it is not just having that smile on a single man face and a pride in their heart.

It is challenging and rewarding at the same time, especially if that single father has support; resilience and not forgetting the well-being of the child, which must come first.

The father will have to come to terms with reality, they now have to share their money with the baby instead of buying additional sneakers; going to lunches, and spending money because they have it in their pockets.

If they do not have job, now will be the time to find one, since they now have responsibilities.

The father will have to understand the navigation of parenting alone, while having to find a home, and managing it, and not forgetting to deal with the emotional stress.

They will have to learn time management by balancing work and parenting, and being able to juggle multiple roles, thereby making sure that they do not get burnt out.

Not forgetting they have to make sure that there is proper communication among the parties who are involved with the child.

THE RESPONSIBILITY OF THE FATHER IN THE HOME

Not all fathers behave the same in their home, sometimes they may imitate the wrong type of dad, and in this case the wrong type of messages or behavior is being passed down from generation to generation.

Some fathers would leave their home in the morning without speaking to the child and return home and say nothing again.

When the child sees this, especially the boy child, he would think it is okay to do so, and when the child gets married, they would want to do the same to their spouse.

Other fathers think that it is okay to treat the spouse in a derogatory manner, and in turn they would do the same to their spouse, and this is done by both girl and boy.

If the child sees the father is interacting, and showing respect, and spending time with their mother, that child will do the same to their family when he gets older or even better.

In most cases one would hear the father say go to your mother, and depending upon another situation the mother would say go to your father. In most cases the father is the one who exercises the authority and make decisions in the household.

The father should know his child friends

Know the child activities.

Have one on one conversations with the child

Be able to identify the challenges of the child

Able to get involve with the daily care of the child if they can

Express affection to both boy and girl

Divide work routine and personal routine by spending some time with the boy and girl

Express affection towards the boy and girl child

Work with partners to collaborate for the children

Get involved in recreational activities

Be consistent in promises

Get involved with the child education

Adapt to the needs of the child

Being able to handle discipline and boundaries.

It is obvious that every child will always want to know as one would say "where they come from" or who is their father. The child will accept a father figure, however there is that desire of who this man is lingers in their mind.

When looking a Jesus Christ, HE was always looking for His father, He was constantly directing his life, prayers, and actions toward God the father. He was acting in perfect submission to divine will, and this is shown in John 5:19; John 5:30; John 6:38; Luke 22:43 and Hebrews 12:2. Mark 1:35 and Luke 5:16.

Father must remember that a child never chooses to come into this world. It is you, the father who is responsible for making the right decision of how you want to bring a child into this world.

Would you deprive the child of enjoying a balancing life?

The responsibility of a father according to the bible

Deuteronomy 6:1-19 New International Version

These are the commands, decrees and laws the Lord your God directed me to teach you to observe in the land that you are crossing the Jordan to possess, [2] so that you, your children and their children after them may fear the Lord your God as long as you live by keeping all his decrees and commands that I give you, and so that you may enjoy long life. [3] Hear, Israel, and be careful to obey so that it may go well with you and that you may increase greatly in a land flowing with milk and honey, just as the Lord, the God of your ancestors, promised you.

[4] Hear, O Israel: The Lord our God, the Lord is one. [a] [5] Love the Lord your God with all your heart and with all your soul and with all your strength. [6] These commandments that I give you today are to

be on your hearts. [7] Impress them on your children. Talk about them when you sit at home and when you walk along the road, when you lie down and when you get up. [8] Tie them as symbols on your hands and bind them on your foreheads. [9] Write them on the doorframes of your houses and on your gates.

[10] When the Lord your God brings you into the land he swore to your fathers, to Abraham, Isaac and Jacob, to give you—a land with large, flourishing cities you did not build, [11] houses filled with all kinds of good things you did not provide, wells you did not dig, and vineyards and olive groves you did not plant—then when you eat and are satisfied, [12] be careful that you do not forget the Lord, who brought you out of Egypt, out of the land of slavery.

[13] Fear the Lord your God, serve him only and take your oaths in his name. [14] Do not follow other gods, the gods of the peoples around you; [15] for the Lord your God, who is among you, is a jealous God and his anger will burn against you, and he will destroy you from the face of the land. [16] Do not put the Lord your God to the test as you did at Massah. [17] Be sure

to keep the commands of the Lord your God and the stipulations and decrees he has given you. [18] Do what is right and good in the Lord's sight, so that it may go well with you and you may go in and take over the good land the Lord promised on oath to your ancestors, [19] thrusting out all your enemies before you, as the Lord said.

Fathers who are in the role of both father and mother.

This multifaceted role can be a mind-bothering situation when the mother of the child is no longer in the home taking on both leadership and discipline role.

The question of "what your mother do when this happens or "what did your mother used to say"

The father now has both responsibilities, for in the beginning it would be tough, however as things get into routine most of the logistics would work out, but the emotional and the nourishing part would be a lack and this is because a father takes role of both mother and father.

This is a heavy task since the instinct of a man is different from the instinct of the woman who is a the nurturer and caretaker.

While the father's responsibility that includes providing for the family; leading the household; and initiating family activities.

This type of father's role is seen as leadership and spiritual guidance. Ephesians 6:4 instructs.

"Fathers, do not provoke your children to wrath; instead, bring them up in the discipline and instruction of the Lord." This verse underscores the father's responsibility to nurture his children in a way that reflects God's teachings, avoiding harshness that could lead to resentment, also the fathers are also called to provide for their families.

In 1 Timothy 5:8 , it is written, «If anyone does not provide for his own, and especially his own household, he has denied the faith and is worse than an unbeliever.» This passage emphasizes the importance of the father›s role as a provider, ensuring the physical and spiritual well-being of his family.

Both parents are called to work together in unity, reflecting the partnership established in Genesis 2:24 : «For this reason a man will leave his father and mother and be united to his wife, and they will become one flesh.» This union is the foundation for a stable and loving environment in which children can thrive Parents are also tasked with teaching their children about God›s commandments and ways.

Deuteronomy 6:6-7 instructs, «These words I am commanding you today are to be upon your hearts. And you shall teach them diligently to your children and speak of them when you sit at home and when you walk along the road, when you lie down and when you get up.» This passage emphasizes the continuous and shared responsibility of both parents to instill a love for God and His Word in their children.

Discipline is a crucial aspect of parenting, and both parents are encouraged to administer it with love and fairness. Proverbs 13:24 states, «He who spares the rod hates his son, but he who loves him disciplines him diligently.» This highlights the importance of corrective guidance as an expression of love, ensuring that children grow up with a clear understanding of right and wrong.

THE FATHER IS A SPIRITUAL LEADER

From the beginning, God holds fathers spiritually accountable for their households.

Deuteronomy 6:6–7 – Teach God's commandments diligently to your children.
• Joshua 24:15 – "As for me and my house, we will serve the Lord."
• Ephesians 6:4 – Bring children up in the training and admonition of the Lord.

The responsibility: of a father is to • Establish worship in the home • Model prayer and obedience • Teach Scripture intentionally • Protect the spiritual atmosphere

A father is not just a provider of income—he is a provider of spiritual direction.

The Father is a Teacher and Trainer
Fathers are commanded to actively instruct.

• Proverbs 22:6 – Train up a child in the way he should go.
• Proverbs 1:8 – Do not forsake your father's instruction.

Responsibility:
• Teach wisdom and discernment
• Correct with patience
• Prepare children for adulthood
• Teach consequences and accountability

Biblical training includes: • Moral guidance • Work ethic • Integrity • Respect

The Father is a Provider and Protector

Scripture clearly teaches material responsibility.

• 1 Timothy 5:8 – If anyone does not provide for his own, he has denied the faith.
• Psalm 127:3–5 – Children are a heritage from the Lord.

Responsibility: • Financial provision • Emotional security • Physical protection • Stability in the home

Provision isn't only money. It includes presence, safety, and emotional coverage.

The Father is a Disciplinarian (With Balance)

Discipline in the Bible is corrective, not crushing.
• Hebrews 12:6 – The Lord disciplines those He loves.
• Colossians 3:21 – Do not provoke your children to discouragement.

Responsibility: Correct sin • Avoid harshness • Balance justice with mercy • Discipline from love, not anger

God's model of discipline is restorative.

The Father in Different Circumstances

Married Father • Lead in unity with your wife
• Love your wife well (Ephesians 5:25) • Model covenant faithfulness Single Father • Rely on God as co-laborer
• Seek wise community support • Stand in both nurturing and leadership roles

Aging Father

• Leave a legacy of faith (Proverbs 13:22) • Bless the next generation • Speak identity into adult children

SPIRITUAL FATHER

Paul describes spiritual fatherhood in: • 1 Corinthians 4:15

Spiritual fathers: • Mentor • Disciple • Encourage growth • Correct in love

The Father is an Image of God

Ultimately, earthly fatherhood points to the heavenly Father.

Jesus reveals God as Father in: • Matthew 6:9 – "Our Father…"

God's fatherhood includes: • Compassion • Forgiveness • Patience • Provision • Covenant love

Earthly fathers reflect Him imperfectly—but intentionally.

Core Biblical Responsibilities Summarized

A biblical father is called to: Lead spiritually; Love sacrificially; Teach intentionally; Discipline wisely; Provide faithfully; Protect consistently; Model integrity; Leave a godly legacy

"Deacon James Donald" – Faith and love Center Pentecostal Church

As a follower of Jesus Christ I know a father is to be the spiritual leader, protector, provider, and teacher of his family.

This also includes discipline and the teaching of our Lord Jesus Christ. As a father I tried to fulfill these aspects. I wanted to be a good father but I often failed because of my disobedience to Christ.

When God blessed me with my daughter it was my opportunity to give all the love I had inside to someone else.

I did all I could to instill in her respect, love, kindness, motivation and of course to follow Christ. I wanted to give her an image of what a good man is and what his role is.

I hoped that she would one day marry someone who has similar character. I believe that a father's role is vital to our child's development and without it children miss key teachings and examples.

"Alvin Matthews"

A father should not be a father in name only. The love that they have in their heart for their child is not enough.

They should take part in the child's life regardless of the situation, because they should definitely want in their child to be better than them.

As a single father it can be difficult at times, and this can be because of a lack of communication; not being able to spend quality time with the child; having to share holidays with the child instead of spending all of it together; and there is the difference in parenting styles.

Not forgetting having to abruptly remove the child from having a great time while playing because they have to go back to the other parents.

All of these can be an hinderance to the child growth, and the father must remember sometime to try to put themselves in the child's shoes and trying to understand what the child feels when have to move from house to house.

Despite all these hindrances the father should make the child a priority in his life and make it their duty to be there for the child.

They should be trustworthy parents not sometimes, but all the time.

"Ako Atikossie"

QUOTES ABOUT THE RESPONSIBILITY OF A FATHER

But God did not create Adam and Eve at the same time. He created Adam first, gave Adam his responsibility. He gave Adam his word. Because God holds men responsible first, when men abandoned their lead responsibility.

Women are critical. They are essential collaborator, But when mankind fell, God didn't come and say Adam and Eve, he said Adam where are you? The Bible says in Adam all die, not an Adam and Eve all died.

When God did the covenant, he said I'm the God of Abraham, Isaac and Jacob not seeing Rebecca and Rachel. In other words, he would hold me and ultimately responsible.

Next to this chapter 34 verses 23 and 24 God called all the males. With all the women home. And he said, if I can get you men to listen to me, I will send you back and I'll save your nation. So, he holds men ultimately responsible.

So, when men fail, it's like the foundation of the house failing. The other parts are critical, but the stability of the other parts are dependent upon the solid foundation.

Foundations don't have to be pretty, but they better be strong.

So, God is calling men to be strong so that everything else, family, churches, and culture can be built on their strength.

Because if not, then we're calling on women to be women and men. He caught his life calling on them to be both.

He's calling Us to be men when men fail, the Bible says in Isaiah chapter 3, when men fail, it says the children rebel, the women take over, and it says the men become weak. So, the Bible holds men ultimately responsible.

"Pastor Tony Evans"

To be the father of growing daughters is to understand something of what Yeats evokes with his imperishable phrase 'terrible beauty.' Nothing can make one so happily exhilarated or so frightened: it's a solid lesson in the limitations of self to realize that your heart is running around inside someone else's body.

Christopher Hitchens, "Hitch 22: A Memoir"

Fathering is not something perfect men do, but something that perfects the man.

"Frank Pittman"

A father is the man who can change a world he will not be part of by building the tiny human that is part of him.

"Craig D. Lounsbrough"

A father is very special, and a very child needs not only the father, but the mother also in their lives, and when it comes to the father when he becomes aware of his responsibility of the child and embraces it whole heart, he will not only show love, he will be present in the child's life all the time.

He will make sure the child wants nothing, he will show love: he will show kindness; he will make sure that every needs for the child are being met.

Regardless of culture of the father, their responsibility for the child is the same.

Some fathers pray daily for their children, something that all fathers should do.

Some fathers go above and beyond in many ways, which is talking to their children; reminding them to live right; to live Christ like, and regardless of what the fathers pray and walk in the foot stops of God.

They are great babysitters and go to the point of supporting their children without judging them. I wish if my dad were here to continue to share his knowledge and wisdom.

"Fabrice Attikossie"

One of the greatest lessons I learned from my dad was to make sure your children know that you love them.

"Al Roker"

When my father didn't have my hand, he had my back.
"Linda Poindexter"

We never know the love of a parent till we become parents ourselves
"Henry Ward Beecher"

The heart of a father is the masterpiece of nature.
"Prevost Abbe, "Manon Lescaut"

Any fool can be a Father, but it takes a real man to be a Daddy.

"Philip Whitmore"

Sometimes the poorest man leaves his children the richest inheritance.

" Ruth E. Renkel"

My father used to say that it's never too late to do anything you wanted to do. And he said, 'You never know what you can accomplish until you try

" Michael Jordan"

My dad was an incredibly brave man, completely dedicated to his family, with a love for all of us. If I can be half the dad he was to me then that will be an achievement in itself.

"Tom Daley"

I'm inspired by the love people have for their children. And I'm inspired by my own children, how full they make my heart. They make me want to work to make the world a little bit better. And they make me want to be a better man." Former President Barack Obama"

Daddies don't just love their children every now and then, it's a love without end.

"George Strait, "Love Without End, Amen"

The call of fatherhood is in fact a call of sacrifice, not in some heroic sense where a father is lifted high on some glowing pedestal with all of his sacrifices held up to the awe of those around him. Rather, it is a call that will cost him all that he has, that will be absent of accolades, where rewards will be sparse, and where he will someday find himself having spent all, but in spending he have gained everything. And this is the glory of fatherhood.

"Craig D. Lounsbrough"

Always a partner, a playmate and a teacher / Ready with a joke when times were sad

" Nancy Sinatra, "It's for My Dad"

Dads are most ordinary men turned into heroes, adventurers, storytellers and singers of song.

"Pam Brown"

Whether a man is married or single, and whether or not he has children, he is designed by God to fulfill the role of father n the lives of those around him. It is his calling to reflect the creative and cultivating nature of God.

Myles Munroe

CONCLUSION

The moral value and responsibility of a father is educational; physical, and creative social communications, and this comes with homework help, reading together, museum visits; sports, outdoor adventures, teaching skills; art projects, music, imaginative play; coaching teams, family gatherings, and community events, and the end results would be evidence of improved academic performance, curiosity; moral development, confidence, health habits ;Problem-solving abilities, self-expression; and Leadership skills, along with empathy, and cooperation.

It is important to understand that not all fathers are the same and will not teach or communicate with their child the same way, also when it comes to the child, some of them will want to act and behave like their fathers, and in many cases it may not be the right thing to do especially if the father does not have a moral life style, or not living the way God intended for them.

Some habits which can be hindrance towards the proper growth for the child will be the lack of communications, abuse, and among other things which can cause great damage, and disrespect to the child, and it would be great idea for the father to think how they would like to be treated, and in turn do the same for your child.

Lastly, the father must remember that the child hurts, just as how they would hurts, they needs hugs and comfort just as how the father need; the child in most cases are taken for granted and the father must always pay special attention, for love is the key.

REFERENCES

Holy Bible

Pleck, J. H. (1997). Paternal involvement: Levels, sources, and consequences. In M. E. Lamb (Ed.), The role of the father in child development (3rd ed., pp. 66-103). New York: Wiley.

Pleck, J. H. (2010). Paternal involvement: Revised conceptualization and theoretical linkages with child outcomes. In M. E. Lamb (Ed.), The role of the father in child development (5th ed., pp. 58-93). New York: Wiley.

Cabrera, N., Fitzgerald, H. E., Bradley, R. H., & Roggman, R. (2007). Modeling the dynamics of paternal influences on children over the life course. Applied Development Science, 11(4), 185-189.

Snider, J. B., Clements, A., & Vazsonyi, A. T. (2004). Late adolescent perceptions of parent religiosity and parenting practices. Family Process, 43(4), 489-502.

Tamis-LeMonda, C. S., & Cabrera, N. (1999). Perspectives on father involvement: Research and policy. Social Policy Report: Society for Research in Child Development, 13(1), 1-32. father involvement and bullying. Aggressive Behavior, 28(2), 126-133

Myles Munroe (Author), John C. Maxwell (2008)The inherent purpose of *all* men is fatherhood.